Sentimental Slop & Haiku

Sentimental Slop & Haiku by MT (Matthew Thomas) Stolte

Copyright © 2021

ISBN: 978-1-7353850-3-7

First Edition

eMTeVisPub

http://www.lulu.com/spotlight/emtevispub

Some of these poems first appeared in *Scars Publications* & *Axe Factory*.

This book was made possible in part by a generous grant from Dane Arts.

DANE ARTS

Engage. Connect. Inspire.

"as sickly a bucket of sentimental slop as was ever scrubbed off the barroom floor." – Gigi Hemingway

"I need some
Sentimental hygiene" – Warren Zevon

for the injured & the discharged

Contents

Introduction

Part 1 – Senti-

Part 2 – mental

Part 3 – Slop

Part 4 – Haiku

Introduction to *Sentimental Slop & Haiku*

I began writing the 1st of these poems in Eugene, Oregon, 1996. I used a red cooler as a table for my Brother electric typewriter & drank beer alone in the bedroom, typing. My wife didn't like that. In 2 years I typed up 4 large 3-ring binders of poems. The original manuscript is titled *Rural Route Narratives*.

Afterwards began nearly 2 decades of throwing most of them away. Stuck in my apartment with an Achilles rupture in 2014, I finally reached the sweet end of the binders. Then 7 more years of editing.

In the meantime, I did write more poems suitable for *RRN* (located in the Senti- & mental parts). Poems not narrative biographical I've collected under the title *Just Poems* (Part 3 – Slop). Haiku makes a 3rd collection. This volume represents the best of the 3 in 4 parts.

Note: The cover image is from a visual poem I made in 2012.

With apologies to the avant-garde.

Part 1 – Senti-

The Black Carriage

There is mystery
in
the theme music to *Mystery!*
in
the voices of
Rigg, Price, Cumming

mystery
in a thin, blue, stitched-sheen hardcover
from my childhood
no moon
but a white attic window
in a black wooden mansion
The Ghost of Windy Hill.

Don't let them
pull over the black
carriage.

Otter

I went to a party
@ a friend's house. @ one point
we were in a room
each telling the others
what animal they'd be
if
they were
one.

One kid
wanted to be a dinosaur;
the others
wanted also
to be
dangerous things.

Before I realized this
I admitted
that I wanted to be
an otter. I have no idea
why. But
it was
true.

Then I was ashamed.

In that moment
it seemed as if
something passed me
by – as if
my classmates
all knew something
else, all
went somewhere
without me.

They

were certainly
on top of
it.

Za

I was born &
lived most of my life
in the dairy state –
Wisconsin.

We were vegetarian
when we were kids –
I remember Mom's
Sukiyaki
from page
145 of
Diet for a Small Planet
a book that inspired a
generation –
including Steve Jobs
born
the same year as my
mother & father: 1955.

As working class kids
we were eligible
for reduced lunch –
that's why I thought
Mom gave up
vegetarianism – the price.

But recently Mom teased
"You wanna know why?
You wanna know why?"

"Why?" I deigned.

"Sausage on pizza."

Great-grandma Win

Olive veins throbbed, hanging
like ropes soaked with
skim milk on the swab deck
like the skim milk
she poured over her cornflakes that sat
in a shallow, white glass saucer all night.
Her eyes rested behind leather sacks
held up by toothpicks

tall & thin
bent in places
like *Sorrow*

flat slippers
polyester pants
Easter pastel blouse
graphite cardigan

I went over on my bike
to play UNO
sit with her
once

she
barely spoke about the bombs
over London.

Cow Poem

Michael Perry
writes about Wisconsin
wrote about
the Pamela Anderson (a.k.a. Gorgeous Babe)
of
cows.

My best farm boy friend
growing up
said

"They have
TWO
holes!"

VCR

I remember
when
VCRs
came out. For my birthday
I requested
special videos
for
my parents to
rent
&
it was
snowy. I remember
the videos I
requested. I was quite
happy
to watch
my
videos on
my
birthday with
my
family.
I was near
high school age
then.

Soon thereafter
(of the advent
of the
VCR)

my parents split up &
videos weren't special
anymore.

The Freshman

I played the guitar
in Band
2
my senior
year. I had
already quit
the biker bar band
by
then.

A freshman
trumpeter
walked down to me
during a break
& said

"How does it feel
to have no chance
at life?"

This was a very shocking
statement. What a little
asshole.

Poem for Laura

She
shared a room
with her
brother: bunk
bed.

One
night
he climbed
on
her
& said
"be
quiet" &
fucked
her.

He fucked her
another
night.

The 3rd
time
she
wouldn't let
him.

They
kept it
secret.

Soon
thereafter he
was playing with a gun with
a
friend
on the couch
&

shot himself in the
face. It
went up his
throat
& out
an eye
ball.

When I
dated her
he still lived
at home
in the trailer on the
farm
working in the
canning plant where
his mom
did. He
was
forever
retarded.

I liked
him. Laura
liked
him. He
was
goofy.

Their father drove
truck
& their
mom
made giant pots of
meaty
spaghetti. Very
very
good.

One day
brother &

sister
got together &
told
mom.

Laura
had a slutty ½
sister whose
father
raped her for
years, creeping
into
the
bed
room at
night, slipping the
small
undies
off. Laura
spent the night
with her
sister
once
&
her
sister's
father
fucked her
too
that
night. The
man
published
a book about his
raping
years
later. Laura
was
in

it.

Bobby

As a baby
he was burned all over.
I think I met him
in kindergarten before
having him as a classmate
7th through graduation.
His hair was spotty – I'm not sure
he had eyebrows or eyelashes
& his eyes rolled dark & oddly
under misshapen eyelids.
His skin was dark red, brown
& flaky, cracked, 100% of it.
I never once thought he was gross or ugly –
he had a sense of humor & was popular
fished & went snowmobiling w/ classmates.
After graduation he worked for a local construction company.

One day soon his girlfriend dumped him.
He sat in a truck
in the driveway of his father's house
& blew his head off.

"W.D.Y.T.o.H.M?"

I asked a college
prof
my 2nd
year

"What do you think
of Henry Miller?"

"I don't think
he's any good," she
replied.

"Why?" I asked.

"Because
I don't think he has anything to say."

I probably said
"Oh," &
walked
out.

Henry Miller
had a lot

to say to
me.

History

The LSD
was still in me.
I was
sitting in my large
history class. Right
before the bell
the female sitting next to me
began to shake
& moan. She was on the floor
violently shaking & moaning
when the bell
rang. This made me
more paranoid.

Same class, a different
late morning
the teacher insisted on
having a question about the Constitution
answered. I knew the answer.
I didn't understand why
no one
answered. She
insisted so I
answered & got it
right: the
government, itself
is considered
a specialist
group.

Those
are the two things I remember
from my history class

before I dropped
out.

American Sandwiches

My grandma
had
white bread
Kraft spread
Oscar Mayer
lunch meat
&
American
singles.

We ate
the sandwich
with potato chips or something
on a white
paper
plate.

I know
it's not healthy, but
it was tasty
&
the memory is good.

I ate
at a table in
France. The father
asked what I ate
in America, suggested
"sandwiches?" &
laughed.

What the hell
do the French
know?

On Burt's Day Off

Burt
stood
at the edge of the bay
before God
before cement and stones
before the trench
before his boys
his boy in one hand
his girl in the other.

This has got to be
some sort of
terror
I knew. A goatee
a blue jean jacket with cotton
lapels and a
cap. Jesus Christ
I thought. He stood there.
His boy wore a red and black
checkered hunting cap and matching
little red coat. Like the *Life*
Kennedy boy
he stood.

I waltzed around the empty bay
looking for
an escape

in my fat, wet plastic pants.

Freer than That

May
nice.

A few clouds in the blue
above the butte finger curling out its houses
partially obscured by firs
cars smoothly pass
boys play Frisbee topless & I cannot hear them
a woman sings operatic songs behind the fully bloomed lilac
& sometimes a violin accompanies
& it
sounds
good
bugs swarm but do not bother me:

I'm investigating the western tanager
darting across tall conifers.

I loiter
& it's even ok
with my gut.

It's all ok it's all ok it's
much
freer
than
that.

Retorts

French wife yelled

"Oh,
why don't you go and eet
a beeg bowl of fucking American Ice
Cream!"

&

"Oh,
why don't you go & leesten to
FUCKING STEREOLAB!"

I
did.

The Departure

She wore black
& fuzzy fleece blue – she
gave them the ticket
turned to me, hugged me
kissed me
& said goodbye. It looked so easy
to walk into that
tunnel.

She nosed up over millions of
pines – south
to San Francisco
then
Charles du Gaul.

I was
sick. I called in
on
time – I felt
better.

In this small town on the coast
people are flowers –
they grow
& stand
there.

The cops are out tonight – it's
Saturday night. I went
to the grocery store
for beer &
bread. Driving home
I saw the cherries go – someone
Marie works with. She had
a headlight out.

That was probably

it.

There is nothing but
a few thousand miles of
moon.

Henry

He sucked me in
by spontaneously
talking about
the Berkley riots.
I sat on the bed
feet to the wet carpet
in front of
the door.

He said
they watched a man
carry heavy stones
to a fire escape
high above a demonstration
one by one
piling
them.

When the man
raised the 1st stone
a sniper
shot him. He said
a lot of things
happened
like that
in those days
just down the coast.

He loved nuked fish
with salsa; I'd bring
a 1.5L bottle of red
& a wine glass
& listen. He'd
recline
with tubes up his
nose. We'd
sleep.

I told him my wife left.
"Your wife," he said
calmly &
articulately
"wasn't good looking
anyway."

He'd
do his pill
routine – a dozen pills
in a mayonnaise cap
next to the television
in the
night.

Part 2 – mental

My Dinosaur Book

I had a green notebook
when I was a kid.
I loved dinosaurs & I traced them
page after page into my notebook
until it was full. I added
the pronunciation in parenthesis
& a small sentence
copied from the book of dinosaurs
as well. I drew a tyrannosaurs
on the back of the notebook
but it wasn't very good.

The teacher asked us
to take out a piece of paper.
I asked around for some paper
but all they did was laugh at me.
"You're stupid", they said,
"You wasted your whole notebook!"
I was ashamed.

Last summer I got sick
& put my car into the ditch.
A policeman went through my box of old stuff
I had left in the back seat.
He made a mess of it.
He probably didn't think anything much
of my dinosaur book either –
my 1st book
the book I made back in 2nd grade.

Witch

Jim could
draw. He'd
poke the paper with the point
of a sharp pencil
and draw a straight
line.
He drew borders
with Middle Eastern designs
aliens & mustard bottles
soda machines, brains that popped
like pop-
corn.

He'd color them
with markers
incorporating inverses & shadow
3 dimensions, the skin of Mars
a Cadillac
the mountains.

He taped them down the hall
& back up
the other
side. Going
from one wall to the
opposite, he'd point
and say
"See".

I came out of
it (my psychosis)
before a quarter panel
of a poster
he'd taped together – 2 blue
figures, outlined
walking beside pines &
a river

dressed in silky PJs
with a witch
of the 60s.

There Should Be a Word

a
noun, for
a fat sparrow
landing on crusty snow.

I Saw a Creature 20 Years Ago

When I think of
my 1st Madison apt.
on Mansion Hill
I see a creature
in there – basement efficiency
who owned an old car &
little else – bought a
blue, vintage couch
to sleep on – painted
on cardboard on cardboard
on the tile floor –
black eyes, white skin, fast
like a mammal you glimpse through the brambles
or
a bird.

SEPT 11, 2001

I had an early class
at the downtown campus
of MATC
(Madison Area Technical College)
8 a.m. - Art History.

Up front
two televisions
like two towers
live –

the instructor
looked at me;
I rolled my eyes.

Then the 2nd
tower
fell.

Wine Song

Wine w/o depression.
Depression w/o wine.
o/w I
I/o w
Iowa.

Ric

They call it a room
but upstairs was really
a rooming house – 4 rooms
1 bathroom.

The room at the end of the hall
across from the bathroom
was the smallest – just room
for a bed & a desk.
Ric lived there one year –
bear-chested & bearded
bear mattress, hot boxing, crack
smoking schizophrenic.
He slept in the hall sometimes
providing a bed for people
he'd meet on the street.
I'd drink with him
carrying over
a 1.5L bottle
of Liebfraumilch.

One day he had a friend over
another schizophrenic (they'd
buttfuck on the bear mattress
in the window
a next-door neighbor told me
"I don't mind what people do
in the privacy of their own home
but I wish they would close the blinds
they'll be up there all night!").

A 3rd man
stopped by the small room
& accepted a glass
of Liebfraumilch.
He took a sip
disappeared into the bathroom

& came back & asked for
another. I poured
another.
He disappeared into the bathroom
again, came back & asked
for another glass.

"Ok, but you've just had two," I said.

"I pour wine for the angels," he replied.

"Well, this is the last one for the angels."

That's how I picked up the habit –
last sip
for the angels.

"You know anything about vampires?"
I asked the friend.

He lay flat on the bed
stiff, as if in a coffin
& said

"& the Dark King says
'You shall rise again
& I shall give you 4-runners
& SUVs...'"

Ric was laughing as his friend
began flopping on the bed
flipping-over & fake fucking it

"& the Dark Lord shall give you women
& bitches & prostitutes..."

"We know how to fuck,"
Ric said.

I still run into Ric
over a decade later

though we haven't said hi
in years.

One night
drinking with Ric
& a runaway couple from Chicago
the young woman a gypsy –
I noticed the window was broken
over the bed
leaving a long crescent-shaped
edge. I
suggested Ric get that fixed
& got a white blanket
for the couple for the night.
As the gypsy lay there
she rubbed her wrists
along the crescent
ended up in the hallway
waving her arms
screaming, spurting blood.
I called 911.

In the morning my blanket
was stuffed in the garbage in back
& it was
orange.

Ric moved out
that year – I would stay
for 3 more
after finally acquiring
my 2-year
liberal arts transfer
associate degree.

The Mole Crab

floating dead
with the clear wave
– mangled white parts –
Kicks!
Cuts-back & burrows.

Nadine

I liked her at 1st sight
& I didn't fuck her.
She was blonde & tan
& I didn't fuck her.
She was just my mom's young age
& I didn't fuck her.
All she wanted was dick
& I didn't fuck her.
She was as wide as tall
& I didn't lay her down.
She showed me pictures of her nude
with her Negro man wearing a white cock cozy
as she lounged in her couch in her robe
drunk
& I didn't fuck her.
Her computer was next to the bed
& I didn't fuck her.
Instead of going to the meeting
she took me to the bars
& I didn't fuck her.
"'cause I'm too fat," she replied to her friend
'cause I didn't fuck her.
I would've fucked her but didn't.
The woman was alive
& I didn't fuck her.
She was mad
& I didn't fuck her.
I painted her portrait
& I didn't fuck her.
She lived with her slow son
who knew her old lovers & I didn't fuck her.
Her apartment contained 2,000 lighthouses
& I didn't blow her foghorn.
She pissed in the sand in the gazebo
as tourists began filing by
& I didn't fuck her.
She never called

& I didn't fuck her.
She fed me
& I didn't.
I spent family Christmas with her
& I didn't.
I'm too young
& I didn't.
It was a laugh
& I didn't.
I don't care that I didn't.
She's gone
now. My
beach
nun.

W/o Wine

W/o wine
it gets late late late.
I get
warm.
I begin to
sink inside.
W/o wine
I own my sleep.

Why does everyone make eye contact
from so far away
w/o wine?

I don't want the same wine
I want some new wine
some good wine
but I don't want wine.

Were you alone when you died?
Were you with wine?
You said, "See how ignorant I am?"
when I told you about
organic wine.

The advice you gave
was, "Stay wet."
Does wine keep you wet
or does wine make you dry?
Is a day w/o sunshine
a day with or w/o wine?

I sleep off my wine.
I water my wine.
I don't drink wine.

une bouteille (one bottle)
all that glass
une nuit sans verre (a night w/o glass)

une nuit chaude de la pierre qui coule
(a hot night of the sinking stone)

Sober Night 2

No booze tonight – beer or wine.
I wanted to bomb my guts
w/ a big stir-fry, spicy
w/ rice & 3 pints of water.
Night comes anyway
sleep comes anyway
midnight comes anyway.
Beer can wait in the fridge
like eggs.
Wine can remain corked & lonely.
I'm not stressed out
& I don't want to get excited.
Sober asleep
my dreams may be sunny
with smiling dogs & cats
& I may see Grandma smiling too.
We'll put pickles in a wagon & walk
       down a dirt road in eternity.

Donation Center

I enjoyed
working at the Donation Center
weekends – weekends
were very busy – it
was the 2nd hardest job
I ever had (the
1st was
washing trucks [semis]
for ex-
loggers).

It was funny when
Angie flattened
cardboard mountain
with a metal baseball bat;
when Darin
greeted customers
wearing a bunny suit;
when I reached for
the CDs in the front seat
of an African American woman's car & she snapped
"Don't you touch my *Graceland*!"
laughing.

Weekends could get so busy
we'd run out of room
for garbage. It's a miracle
I wasn't splayed. People
left the job to go back
to working hazmat
or
cleaning military
disaster areas.

One man
donated a toaster –
"Only one side

works," he said.
Another
donated a gun case.
"Is there a gun in it?"
the attendant asked.
"No!" the donor said &
sped off. There was.
One day the police came
with cart after cart
of donations – all from a room
from an apartment
of one of the retail
managers – she'd
take one or two things home
each day
in her
backpack. Another manager
took photos of little girls
changing
& uploaded the photos
to the office computer.

I itched my face
growing a beard
with my work gloves on &
had strange acne
on my cheeks
for a year.

I found
a 50
in the underside of a
jewelry box lid
& turned it in.

It was HOT
in the summer &
COLD
in the
winter.

Sometimes I had to walk
a ½ mile
to the nearest
bus, or
FROM
the nearest bus
to GET to work. I
made the mistake of
getting a ride to work
from the new guy with
narcolepsy.

When I was promoted
without any say in the matter
I was sad
to go. December 31st –
that was
it.

Terrence

He was fun
to work with;
he gave me a ride home
from the grocery store.

I recognized him on TV;
saw his headshot
black & white
in the paper in the cafeteria.

The young man he shot died.

2 lbs. of weed
in a bright, child's backpack

I see Terrence I see
bars.

Pain & Death

W/ my fresh Achilles tendon rupture
a taxi driver told me about his surgery –
tumors, benign, though painful, under his face.
He had the doctors photograph the operation –
he thought it was great

"When else could I bitch slap
my own face with my face?"
he said.

I got out of the taxi
feeling less pain.

I called my boss –
she said a friend of hers
had a blood clot in her hand –
1st the fingers went numb
then they amputated
the hand.

Another taxi driver
said a friend of his was hit by a car as a child
& never outgrew the trauma –
blowing all the money from court
on booze & loans to friends & junk.

I was diagnosed
with DVT & spent the evening
in ER. I've
been receiving calls all day
from every office I can imagine,
offices
I didn't know existed.
It dawned on me
that people are concerned
of my death.

Death prevention –
the great
coordination.

Apples & Green Grapes @ the Food Pantry

Americans
    (in the food pantry anyway)
must forget
    the sweetness of fruit.
I packed my lunch
    a container too full
for a thin slice of apple
    & a green grape –
I set it aside
    grape on slice
Japanese style?
    for breakfast.
Creamy & sweet
    as a French puff pastry –
People at the pantry
    are asked if they'd like fruit
& say
    "No".

WI August Wildflowers & National Guard

Goldenrod tassels sway
bobbing Black-eyed Susans –

"Tell me ye sailors, tell me true
Does my Sweet William sail with you?"

Queen Anne's lace
from Afghanistan to
Saint Anne, mother of Mary, grandmother of Jesus;
Queen Consort Anne of Denmark.

Sunflower, Joe-Pye Weed, Bull Thistle
Bee Balm, Coneflower & Loosestrife

across the street from the National Guard's
camouflaged jeeps & desert sand trucks
fenced-in, restricted, drug free zone with its
Susans, Joes & Queens.

Whitetail cross the street –
a doe & 2 fawns
a doe & a fawn lagging
walking cautiously along the fence.

Ernest

Ernest lived upstairs.
One day he knocked on my door.
He liked my guitar playing.
"You play bass?" I discovered.
I'd take my amp & guitar up
with a few beers – Ernest
sat on his bass amp.
I played his bass once
& my hand hurt for a week.
I saw his ass
the 2nd time he fell
down the stairs
& I saw his penis
when he came back from the bathroom –
it
flopped about like a brown
fish – "I gotta go," I said.
Ernest was blind
& an alcoholic.
The last time I saw him
I gave him my last 19 oz.
The last time we played
for a small, home audience, whew
we were
great.

The Man with the Shoe

I saw a man today
@ Saint Vincent's
wearing a backpack
as a right
shoe. He
smelled ½ like urine
& ½ like something else. He
laughed as I
dug for
vinyl.

The transgender manager said
"I don't think yr funny"
& offered him
$35 worth of
undergarments.

I found acid house
Bob Dylan
Grace Jones
a couple soundtracks
& more until
my back hurt.

The bearded man
in the long, gray, summer coat
laughed near me
as I
mined

1 time
2 times
3

wearing a bright, blue backpack
as a
shoe.

Hiking in Black River State Forest Early Spring 2021

Burgundy buds, forest green needles
Gray rock face, mint lichen on gray bark
Misty itty mist ethereal –

    no, not thunder
Cannons at Fort McCoy.

WI Tamarack

sole, bright burnished gold, scraggly
      WI native tamarack on the side of the road
head in the wires

      against a stand of taller green pines
hotter summers, colder winters
      insects
tamaracks drown

Part 3 – Slop

Slip Away, Salamander

The poem
can slither through the bilge
the sewer
the spew &
the sandman &
socks

of the underground
mind.

Good Poetry

The best thing to do
in a poem
is
get
out.

Booze & Creativity

When I moved into a cabin w/o a refrigerator
a friend asked

"How will you keep your beer cold?"

"I'll drink red wine," I replied.

"Good attitude," he said.

Now that I have neither beer nor wine
I am not inspired to paint.
So I work on poems.

Upright

Some poet wrote
books stand like soldiers
on shelves. I hate that.
I rearranged some shelves this afternoon
& the books are clean, pressed
together, one by
one ready
to tip from the row by finger
to be
read. They're not
soldiers.

Soldiers
are unread books
used to hit people on the head.

Service

Pissing the shit
off the inside of toilet bowls
is my little, manly service
to humanity.

Animals Poem

after *Silly Goofball Pomes* by Jack Kerouac

A snake is a worm-animal.
A dog just walks around.
Cats pilot star ships.
Red & black boxelder bugs come in to get warm.
Scutigera coleoptrata I haven't seen upstairs.
Bats upside down flit inter-dimensionally the shape of
        groundcherry wrappers.
Birds quiet come fall all winter trip.
Butterfly like bat flat.
Worms a flat battlefield wet.
Whitetail neither an office designed
nor automatic double doors.
Coyote a wolf dog.
Wolf, the wild.
Sandhill group play front yard.
Blue heron in stream like mentally ill man in bathroom.
Turtle an ancient solar panel.
Spider, O spider, just not cute

or if was
butte.

How to Make Hash Browns

There are 2 secrets
in making hash browns:

    #1 rinse the shredded potato
    #2 don't pat them down when
    you place them in the frying pan.

I'm mostly vegan now
but when I 1st moved to
Madison, WI
I lived on:

    whitetail liver
    onions
    potatoes.

I'd have cereal for breakfast
(or granola & yogurt
if I was lucky to have
had a relative buy me a bag
of groceries – I became
savvy w/ food pantries)
though one morning I had to
eat it w/ a fork as
my junky friend stole all my
spoons.

I had a never-ending string
of temp jobs, little jobs
bigger jobs, &
several years of taking
classes, resulting in
at least
an associate degree –

popping
generous amounts of prescribed

mental health medications
binge drinking daily
(my peak was
4 1L bottles of Liebfraumilch a day)
having 1 diminishing in intensity
episode of psychosis a year
from 1998 thru 2004
(brief relapse in 2010)
finalizing my divorce
(she was on the line
at lunch
in a phone booth in
Paris)
painting daily, finally
in 2004
selling my car, dropping
out of school & beginning work
for a South Central Wisconsin
non-profit, only
having had 1 girlfriend
briefly
the entire
time

infrequently
being dragged out of my apt.
by police
arrested
jailed
turned away from
mental health services
when I was off
insurance.

My point is this:
2 police cars
just left with
a woman from upstairs –
not me. I
had my breakfast
working on this poem.

"Things work out," a celebrity
said on television last night.
It's not so difficult.
Make hash browns for breakfast.

Get on Your Bicycle

GET ON YOUR BIKE
you fuddy-duddy conservative.
GET ON YOUR BIKE
dusty man; fat woman.
GET ON YR BIKE
or take a hike.

GET ON YR BIKE
It's cold? Put clothes on.
GET ON YR BIKE
to work, shop, school.
GET ON YR BIKE
for no reason.

GET ON YR BIKE
you gluttonous slob.
GET ON YR BIKE
infinite consequences.
GET ON YR BIKE
Ride the Winter Garden.

Bus Meditation

Bus Meditation x 2

Where suddenly race is proportionate;
Where beautiful women sit;
Someone's coughing in it.

Bus Meditation x 2

My feet are cold in it;
Sometimes there's nowhere to sit;
Pot, beer & sex odor emits.

Bus Meditation x 2

There's no room for my bike;
Fares took another hike;
Strollers, wheelchairs & shopping carts like.

Bus Meditation x 2

No indoor stations;
No posted time information;
Bitter cold patience.

Bus Meditation

Junk Lyrics

Fistula & abscess;
gotta work gotta rest.

Taco, Paco
diarrhea, loco.

New Deli asphalt melt
sea stars smelt.

No coral relief
so you can Drive Thru for treats?

My poverty
yr unreachable novelty.

Visor foggy
baby froggy dropped his doggy;
3D camera biopsy drowsy.

No food, water, table;
earth uninhabitable.

Replete with staples
music's 4 squares stable.

Do 2 in tin
really got a gin?

More words than K/curds
bees, birds, brew, butter

bike chains & up water.

Poem-y Poem

My brain is mush-y mush
Our butts tush-y tush
Bush-y bush & brush-y brush
I should just shush-y shush

Drank & had to leak-y leak
Friend died & weep-y weep
Weeks go by week-y week
Beer 4 is sleep-y sleep

Went to work-y work
Boss spoke terse-y terse
I called her a jerk-y jerk
This is my universe-ety verse-y verse

We used a map-ety map
Arrived & nap-ety napped
Our love sacrosanct-ety sacrosanct
We split like that-ety that

Elon Musk-ety Musk
Mark Zuckerberg-ety Zuck
Stormy Daniels-ety Dusk
Donald Yuck-ety Yuck

Up all night-y night
Afraid asshole tight-y tight
If I may I might-y might
We are wrong & we are right-y right

Tennyson poetry denizen-y denizen
Austin Powers & Dr. Evil cryogenically frozen-ety frozen
Too cold dip yr toes-ety toes in
You can't do it unless yr binge-ety binge'n

Is Tonto really an Indian-y Ingine?
Monet really stand by the engine-y engine?

66

Einstein draft the equation-y 'quation?
Mastodons on earth stand-ety stand'n?

Miley Cyrus singing NSFW unicorn horn on
Star wand, fake breasts & strap-ety strap-on
200 million $s & dong-ety dong
All that fame & I don't know 1 song-ety song

Suddenly women wear purple-y purple
Force rhymes until they work-ety workle
A co-worker was a curple-y curple
Reinvent the wheel goggling in circle-y circles

Juggling jester with orange-y orange
Actors order duck a l'orange-y l'orange
Perfumed mall store of lingerie-y linge'
Try to rhyme orange students cry c'mon-ety c'monge!

Empty-ety empty
Have empathy-ety empathy
Eat beans-ety beans-y
Dream dreams-ety dreams-y

1st Letter Pwitch Soem

a dit brunk
tlittle aired

aalling fsleep
tungry & hhirsty

lad & sonely
dweaty & sirty

cresh & flean
rell wested

aide wwake

Yes I've poished some publems!

I've had drain bamage ever since Bavid Dowie died!

I'm going for a ralk before the wain.

Incense Poem for JMB

Copious Copal JMB
Sudden Eel Dragons Blood
(Dragon's Dragons') Drag
JM Bee Sting Sob Sod
Sudan. Sodden heel.
reed taint. lean abate.
SM el
el

M
out was ash

From *The World Without Us*

yr not supposed to eat
the spider-monkey meat

Marsh Butter

Biking between rain bombs for bouteilles du rouge in the obscene
Anthropocene

Goldenrod crab spiders alter their coloration

Octopuses cytoelastic sacculi are filled with pigment in each chromatophore

Boy George drops his signature androgynous look for a night out.

Part 4 – Haiku

The big metal mixing bowl
        we puked in, also
was used for popcorn & bread.

                              Not purple, Spring flowers –
                                    a big, empty aluminum can
                              on brown, roadside leaves.

Neighbors shouting at their dogs
        to be quiet
are much louder than the dogs.

Spring cold –
      landlord turned the heat off;
employer turned the air on.

           October Queen Anne's lace
              like-new
      as if nothing was rotten all around
              it.

Young woman in a neon peach
tank
      running, running across the
      wide intersection
late for morning yoga.

That moon
        makes NHQ
small.

In between the mountains
        and the clouds –
the mountains.

Startled by a yellow sac spider
        reaching up to my coffee
        mug from the coaster –
1st snow.

Notes on the Poems

The Ghost of Windy Hill 1968 by Clyde Robert Bulla, Illustrated by Don Bolognese.

Poem for Laura December 14, 2005.

My Dinosaur Book April 9, 1999. Published online by Scars Publications, http://scars.tv/cgi-bin/framesmain.pl?writers.

The Mole Crab July 2002, Charleston SC.

W/o Wine December 9, 2013.

Terrence November 4, 2012.

Slip Away, Salamander published in Axe Factory #11, 1999.

Booze & Creativity April 6, 2016.

Animals Poem October 2012. After Jack Kerouac's poem *Silly Goofball Pomes*, collected in Pomes All Sizes & Collected Poems. Also performed by Juliana Hatfield on the album Kerouac – Kicks Joy Darkness.

Get on Your Bicycle January 23, 2013.

Bus Meditation January 4, 2014.

Incense Poem for JMB June 2019. JMB is John M. Bennett. Written in Madison, WI, after a visit trading incense & cheese.

From the World Without Us 2007 by Alan Weisman.

MT Stolte – Madison WI – July 20, 2021

Selected books by MT Stolte

Concrete Dollars & Cents Poems
Construction Paper Poems
Magnetic Poems

Books by John M. Bennett & MT Stolte

Drilling for Suit Mystery
Jem Tabs Trace

This is eMTeVisPub #15

eMT Evis Pub 2021

www.ingramcontent.com/pod-product-compliance
Lightning Source LLC
Chambersburg PA
CBHW081544040426

42448CB00015B/3211